The Carnivore Code Bible 2023

365 Days Of Tender & Delicious Recipes To Unlock The Secrets Reclaim Your Health, Strength, And Vitality By Returning To Our Ancestral Diet

Blake Reed

TABLE OF CONTENTS

INTRODUCTION

You want to give a carnivore diet a shot since you've heard that some individuals have found significant gains on it, from weight reduction to depression and anxiety to autoimmune illness. You've found the right thing. In this book, we will discuss a few different approaches to the carnivore diet and provide some example meal plans for the carnivore diet to assist you in getting started with the diet.

The first question you need to ask yourself is what you hope to accomplish with this diet, and then you should consider how well it fits in with your lifestyle.

In the meal plans that follow, I have proposed meals for breakfast, lunch, and dinner; however, eating only once or twice a day is entirely acceptable and might even be preferable!

In contrast to other diets, which detail exactly how much food to consume and when to consume it, a carnivore diet does not specify when or how much food one must consume. You can only choose from a minimal selection of foods if you follow this plan.

To prepare for this diet, you must consider how well you can handle following an incredibly restricted eating plan. It is in your best interest to evaluate how well you will be able to stick to this method of eating consistently because it can also be challenging to follow in social situations, such as while dining in a restaurant or at family gatherings.

CAN MEAT FIT INTO A HEALTHY DIET?

The meat debate is both complicated and divisive. Nutrition experts have sent mixed messages for years. The conversations are not only about meat's direct health effects but also its environmental effects. There are reasons to eat meat and avoid it, but few people can agree on what it does for our bodies or how it affects the planet. Some people consider meat a fantastic source of nutrients, while others argue that it harms human health. For every claim that meat might cure a chronic illness, there seems to be another claim implying that meat causes heart disease and cancer. Some sources say meat is environmentally-friendly, and others say meat production contributes to deforestation. This article attempts to untangle the meat debate from a health-based perspective and uncover the pros and cons of eating meat.

The argument over meat is contentious and complicated. For years, nutritionists have given contradictory advice. Not only are the environmental effects of meat discussed, but also its direct effects on health.

Few people can agree on precisely what meat does for our bodies or how it affects the planet, but there are reasons to eat it and avoid it. While some claim that meat is a fantastic source of nutrients, others claim it is unhealthy for people's health.

There seems to be a claim implying that meat causes heart disease and cancer for every claim that it might treat a chronic illness.

HOW DIFFERENT CULTURES DEFINE MEAT

Meat refers to the flesh and other parts of animals, such as mammals and birds, that humans consume after they have been prepared.

The term "meat" generally refers to the fatty tissue and muscle tissue of mammals and birds in the United States and many other countries. However, "meat" can also refer to other edible tissues, such as organs.

Offal-The liver, kidneys, brains, and intestines of animals were traditionally consumed as food in many different civilizations throughout history. On the other hand, it has experienced a decline in popularity in several Western regions. Even today, people from many different cultures worldwide enjoy eating offal, particularly those from more traditional societies.

Additionally, many delicacies use organs. A traditional French delicacy made from duck or goose liver is foie gras. Menudo is a traditional meat dish in Mexico that includes beef stomachs (tripe) and meat in broth. Sweetbreads are made of meat from the thymus gland and have been consumed in Europe since the Roman era.

Nowadays, farms are where meat is produced. Most commercial meat products are made from domesticated animals kept in sizable industrial facilities, where hundreds or thousands of animals may be housed simultaneously. However, in some traditional societies, hunting is the only means of obtaining meat.

In general, meat is consumed after it has been cooked and occasionally after it has been cured or smoked. It is most consumed in steak, chops, ribs, or roast; however, it is also available in powdered or ground forms.

You can cook meat in or serve it with a sauce, condiment, or side dish, all of which can be dipped into the juices left over from cooking the meat.

TYPES OF MEAT WE CAN EAT

The meat classification considers the type of animal the meat originates from and how it is prepared.

RED MEAT

Myoglobin, a protein high in iron that is only found in mammals, is present in red meat in more significant quantities than in white meat. These are a few instances:

Lamb, veal, beef (cattle), pork (pigs and hogs), and (calves)

Goat-based meats like venison, bison, and elk (deer)

WHITE MEAT

In contrast to red meat, which is dark in color before and after cooking, white meat is described as lighter. Even though some birds' flesh isn't red, like in the case of a duck, the expression frequently refers to all birds. Other instances include chicken, turkey, goose, and wild birds like quail and pheasants.

PROCESSED MEAT

Processed meat is a red or white meat that has been "treated" in some way. It may be enhanced or preserved in various ways, such as drying, smoking, curing, salting, and other techniques. Some examples include hot dogs, sausage, and bacon meats like pastrami, salami, and jerky.

HEALTHY WAYS TO EAT MEAT

Many people worried about their hearts and waistlines have recently sharpened their steak knives after learning that eating a little red meat doesn't always put you on the fast track to Fat Central. It's not the meat you want to limit; it's the aged, artery-clogging, cholesterol-rising saturated fat in the meat. This is how:

1. Pick the best one. When shopping for meat, choose cuts with the USDA Select grade label. They have less fat than Choice and Prime.

2. Get slim. Choose packages that say "lean" or "extra lean." Lean meat has less than 8.5 grams of fat per 3-ounce serving. Extra-lean meat has less than 4 grams of fat per 3-ounce serving.

3. Don't leave the grass. Try to buy meat that says it was "grass-fed" or "raised on pasture." It might have 25% to 50% less fat, fewer calories, and more omega-3s, which are suitable for your heart, than regular grain-fed meat. It also means that the animal was raised kindly.

4. Start cutting. Trim any fat from the outside before you cook it, and use that sharp knife to cut off any fat that's still there once it's cooked. This can cut the fat you eat by as much as half.

Keep it separate. Meat can be roasted, grilled, or broiled on grills or pans that drain fat.

Dry off. After cooking, blot meatballs and hamburgers with paper towels to remove grease and calories.

Know your limitations. Real Age advises only one serving of red meat per week. According to the USDA, one serving is the equivalent of a deck of cards or about 3 ounces.

WHAT ARE THE MOST COMMON MISCONCEPTIONS ABOUT THIS DIET

WE NEED PLANTS FOR COMPLETE NUTRITION

Protein, vitamins, and minerals are plentiful in plant-based foods. They have numerous health advantages and are undoubtedly a good source of nutrients. However, plants do not offer a complete diet. Although they are a rich source of nutrients, plants also lack some crucial ones.

Certain nutrients are necessary but are not supplied by plants. These nutrients include vitamin D, typically in animal-derived foods like fatty fish such as cholecalciferol (vitamin D3). Compared to the plant form of vitamin D, it aids in increasing vitamin D levels (D2).

Only meat, particularly red meat, contains heme iron. Compared to non-heme iron found in plant sources, it is an excellent source of iron. The body can more easily absorb heme iron.

An essential omega-3 fatty acid called docosahexaenoic acid (DHA) is typically present in fish oil and fatty fish. It is necessary for the growth and operation of the brain.

Because it contains all nine essential amino acids, meat is a complete nutrition food. Iron, minerals, and vitamins A and B12 are all abundant in meat. Additionally, it has a high concentration of choline, a nutrient that promotes the health of the liver, muscles, and brain.

FIBER IS IMPORTANT FOR GUT HEALTH

Since a carnivore diet excludes all plant foods, it lacks fiber. So, do you need to eat more fiber? Or are any supplements recommended? No, you don't need to increase your intake of fiber. Unexpectedly, recent studies claim that fiber is not a necessary nutrient.

As you might expect, many people may experience significant changes in their bowel habits because of this. Of course, fiber is not necessary for a healthy digestive system. Fiber influences bowel function and may be the root of some digestive issues. Reabsorbing water is one of the colon's main jobs. In a diet high in plant-based foods, fiber performs most of the colon's functions, including absorbing water and creating bulk and consistency in the stools, which causes the colon muscle to weaken.

The amount of fiber you eat drastically changes when you switch from a plant-based diet to a carnivore diet. The muscles in the colon need some time to regain strength because they are not being used and have become weak. You may have loose stools for the first few days. It might take a few weeks for the colon to recover its capacity.

Because meat is absorbed reasonably in your small intestine, all the nutrients are utilized.

Fiber benefits the intestinal flora. It promotes the development of bacteria, which then ferment and release gas. It's possible that eliminating fiber from our diet won't help the bacteria. Our bodies' microbiomes communicate by sending signals like increased appetite and hunger. The benefits of fiber for microbiomes are poorly understood, so it is unclear how these microbes function.

There aren't many ongoing studies that mention adding dietary fiber to meat products. Numerous properties may be improved, including water retention, emulsion stability, texture modification, and neutral flavor. These are all still in the research phase without any conclusive evidence.

Studies have also shown that cutting back on dietary fiber may help to lessen constipation and its signs and symptoms. Therefore, there is insufficient evidence to establish the necessity of fiber for regular bowel and gut functions.

RED MEAT SHORTENS OUR LIFE AND CAUSES CANCER

Beef, veal, pork, lamb, mutton, horse, and goat are examples of red meat. Meat comes in two varieties: processed meat and unprocessed meat. Salt, fermentation, smoking, and curing processes are used to improve the flavor and preservation of processed meat. They consist of ham, salami, sausages, bacon, and salami. While all fresh, minced, and frozen beef, pork, and lamb are considered unprocessed meat. Fresh white meat from fish and chicken is not related to increased cancer risk. The chemicals in processed meat include hazardous substances like haem, nitrates and nitrites, heterocyclic amines, and polycyclic amines. By harming our cells, these chemicals may raise the risk of developing cancer. Consuming 300 to 500g of cooked meat daily carries no cancer risk. Additionally, consuming processed meat in moderation can reduce the risk of developing cancer.

Some advice on how to lower one's cancer risk.

> Consume moderately: An average daily intake of red meat of 70 grams is recommended. Consuming red meat in moderation can help reduce the risk of developing cancer, so cutting it out entirely is unnecessary.
> Change to white or fish meat instead of red. Additionally, you can eat this dish with less red meat.
> Try to go without red meat twice a week.

According to a recent study, eating fish regularly can help lower your risk of developing stomach cancer. Despite the abundance of evidence linking processed foods to cancer, it has been noted that unprocessed red meat poses no health risks. Think ahead and incorporate alternate meat options into your diet.

RED MEAT CAUSES CARDIOVASCULAR DISEASE

During digestion, red meat excretes large quantities of nutrient-associated compounds. It is considered that the high quantities of saturated fat in red meat contribute to cardiovascular disease.

Few studies suggest that Trimethylamine N-oxide (TMAO), a byproduct of Red meat, is high in protein and iron that is readily absorbable. Red meat is considered to cause heart disease, although there is insufficient data to support this theory.

Consumption of red meat digestion produced by gut bacteria may increase cholesterol deposits in the arterial wall. Extreme consumption of TMAO, which interacts with blood cells and is essential for clotting reactions, may raise the risk of stroke and heart attack.

Research shows no link between unprocessed meat consumption and cardiovascular disease risk or blood pressure. The presence of preservatives and visible fat in processed meat are the primary causes of increased heart risk.

According to another study, daily consumption of 70g of red meat does not affect blood lipids, lipoproteins, or blood pressure. There is no link between white meat and fish and cardiovascular disorders. Although there is evidence that processed meat raises the risk of cardiovascular disease, unprocessed meat is believed to be safe. Eating red meat in moderation has no health risks.

WHAT IS THE CARNIVORE DIET?

It's easy to follow a carnivorous diet; all your food comes from animals. Everything else has limitations. No fruits, vegetables, bread, grains, and low-lactose dairy products are allowed. It nearly goes against the grain of a vegan diet.

Although it might initially sound absurd, some people believe that plant foods are unnecessary for survival. The only non-essential macronutrient is carbohydrates in large quantities in plants. This indicates that while our bodies need fats and proteins to survive, we don't require carbs similarly.

The carnivore diet is a kind of evolution of the keto and paleo diets. It is based on the debatable notion that high-carb diets are to blame for the prevalence of chronic inflammation, disease, and gastrointestinal problems in Western countries and America because our predecessors mostly consumed meat and fish.

By consuming only foods derived from animals, the Carnivore Diet, a contentious progression of the keto and paleo diets, seeks to eliminate carbohydrates from your diet. progression of the keto and paleo diets, seeks to eliminate carbohydrates from your diet.

FOODS YOU CAN EAT ON THE CARNIVORE DIET

Carnivorous diet foods include:

Eggs give the proper quantities of protein, lipids, and nutrients for a carnivorous diet, helping your body work well.

Bone broth helps carnivores' intestines, skin, and joints.

Grass-fed meat should provide the most calories, especially fatty cuts like NY strip steak, ribeye, pork chops, porterhouse, bacon, 80/20 minced beef, T-bone, and flank steak. Your body can use high-fat foods as energy because you're eating fewer carbohydrates.

Choose the fattiest fish you can find, like beef, trout, mackerel, catfish, salmon, sardines, and other fish are okay.

Low-lactose dairy products A large percentage of carnivores acquire lactose intolerance.

Use lard, grease, and other animal fats instead of vegetable oil.

The carnivore diet allows simple seasonings, sauces, and flavors. Pepper, salt, spices, and herbs are examples. Use low-sugar, low-carb ingredients whenever possible. Adding calorie-free hot sauce to meat can increase flavor.

THE BEST TIPS FOR THOSE CONSIDERING BEGINNING THE CARNIVORE DIET

You may get confused regarding the carnivore diet, as it's a different concept. And you might be a little unsure about the specifics of the Carnivore Diet if you're considering starting it. So, sharing some valuable tips about the carnivore diet

Get used to not needing plants.

When it comes to protein, there are no plant-based foods. Dairy has occasionally been included in diets; this is optional but may provide your meals with a little more diversity than meat.

Three meals per day?

You can eat three meals a day consistently or try the even more recent fad of intermittent fasting, depending on your weight loss goals.

Hot beverages

Tea and coffee could be included in your diet as additional items to spice things up. Make sure not to include any sugar, though.

I have an uncommon one!

Cook the meat as you usually would, depending on taste, although rare to medium rare is recommended (when talking about red meat).

All meat types are healthy meat types.

Red and white meat, whole eggs, dairy products, and bone marrow should all be on your list of acceptable carnivore foods.

The organs from meats (such as the heart and liver) and bone broth should be utilized. Particularly organ meats contain more micronutrients than veggies.

Athletes should wait for outcomes with patience.

Athletes should be aware that it will take their bodies about six months to adjust to this strict diet. Diet adjustments may be necessary for high-performing athletes depending on their body's needs. Although theoretically forbidden by the diet, vegetables like broccoli, cauliflower, and kale may occasionally need to be added. Apples and sweet potatoes are the most effective choices for pre-exercise energy.

Fat in beef

Try to make beef your primary source of fat when on a diet. Consider the following cuts for variety: roasts (prime rib, chuck, brisket), ground beef, and steaks (ribeye, sirloin, strip, and chuck eye).

Fewer Snacks and Larger Meals

If you feel hungry and have the urge to snack, eat larger meals or more frequently throughout your diet.

THE CARNIVORE DIET FOOD PYRAMID

As you might guess, the food pyramid for someone following the Carnivore Diet differs slightly from the standard pyramid. Bread, cereal, and rice are at the base of a classic food pyramid, with fats, oils, and sweets at the very top. Comparing a regular food pyramid to a Carnivore Diet food pyramid is intriguing due to the place of meat. Traditional diets place meat, poultry, and fish at the second-highest rung of the pyramid, corresponding to about two daily portions. This is completely reversed in the Carnivore Diet food pyramid, which places meat and eggs at the bottom and recommends eating them whenever you feel hungry. This means that they are the foundation of your diet; everything revolves around your regular meat consumption.

When looking at the food pyramid, you may come across what many consider to be the main barrier to trying the Carnivore Diet. Where's everything else to eat but meat and eggs? If you want to start putting together a carnivore diet meal list, your variance will come more from the meats you choose than from how colorful your dishes are with veggies and greens.

On the other hand, the diet does expressly cater to a fitness-based clientele by permitting energy snacks and supplements. However, once more, they should all appear as natural as possible.

FOODS TO AVOID ON THE CARNIVORE DIET

We are now entering the challenging phase. You can no longer eat many of the snacks and meals that you normally eat if you eat like a carnivore.

Carnivores cannot eat the following:

Every fruit: bananas, apples, berries, tomatoes.

Every veggie: Vegetable sauces and vegetable broth are included.

Majority of dairy products: The amount of dairy you consume is dubious among carnivores. While most people prefer aged cheeses and kefir over creamy cheeses and yogurt, low-lactose options are preferred as well.

Every sugar: All added sugars are prohibited! Natural sugars are also subject to the same rules.

Every additive: processed foods, especially frozen and canned foods, that contain additives like MSG, nitrates, and nitrites.

Low-quality meat: Though meat is the main focus of the carnivore diet, this does not mean any meat is served at meals. If you want to prevent inflammation caused by grains, you must consume grass-fed and pasture-raised meats.

All grain, bread, pastry, etc.: Neither grains nor bread are allowed! Rice and pasta are excluded from this list.

All seeds, legumes, and nuts: All nuts, seeds, and legumes are also prohibited. Almonds, peanuts, chia seeds, flax seeds, and flax oil are among the foods that are high in omega-3 fatty acids.

Whatever else isn't meat! Meat substitutes such as Beyond Burgers, confections like taffy, and meat produced in laboratories come under this category.

THE HYPOTHESIS BEHIND THE CARNIVOROUS CLAIMS

The main argument used by proponents of a carnivorous diet is that plants are harmful to people because they contain substances that are toxic to animals.

For instance, the most heavily defended plant foods are nuts and seeds. They contain substances that have the potential to cause immunological responses and nutrient deficits.

Contrarily, meat is devoid of these potentially harmful substances. Instead, you receive complete proteins, healthy fats, and highly available minerals.

With this knowledge, it might seem clear that we should limit plant-based foods. But in doing so, we would have to disregard the overwhelming body of research demonstrating the health advantages of whole plant diets, including those strongly advocated.

A carnivore diet may benefit a limited subset of individuals with autoimmune disorders or digestive problems brought on by plants, but this does not imply that it is the best course for everyone. There are several gray areas to consider choosing the best course of action for you, just like with any other diet.

GOLDEN RULE OF THE CARNIVORE DIET

- Consume solely foods made from animals.
- Keep up a low-carb diet

If meat is the only thing you eat, you should be fine (the all-meat diet). Because they are derived from animals, dairy products are permissible, although the first signs of carbs start to appear on the nutritional labels beyond this point.

You'll notice that we split dairy foods into two categories: those low in lactose and those high in lactose. This is because lactose, also referred to as milk sugar, is the type of sugar that may be found in milk. What does sugar mean? CARBS! a definite no-no.

Therefore, if you want to follow the Carnivore Diet in the letter, you should avoid consuming dairy products with high lactose concentrations. It is ultimately up to you to decide how much you should limit your consumption of low-lactose dairy products.

To be of some assistance to you, we have compiled the following list of average carbohydrate counts per serving found in everyday dairy products.

CARBOHYDRATES PER OUNCE IN CARNIVORE-FRIENDLY DAIRY PRODUCTS

- Ghee contains no carbohydrates per ounce
- Butter contains no carbohydrates per ounce
- In one ounce of Brie, there are 0.1 grams of carbohydrates
- Cheddar cheese has 0.4g of carbohydrates per ounce
- There are 0.6g of carbohydrates in an ounce of mozzarella cheese
- In one ounce of heavy cream, there are 0.83 grams of carbohydrates
- There are 0.9g of carbohydrates per ounce in Parmesan cheese
- Each ounce of cream cheese contains 1.2 grams of carbohydrates
- Half & Half contains 1.3g of carbohydrates per ounce

HOW DO CARNIVORES WORK?

The goal of a carnivore diet is to consume as little carbohydrates as possible—basically none—while consuming a lot of protein and fat. This is achieved by limiting foods.

Low-carb diet meal plans frequently limit the number of plant-based foods available because carbohydrates are found in anything that grows above ground (also known as plants). The strictest diet, called carnivore, forbids the consumption of plant-based products, including seeds, nuts, and non-starchy vegetables that are common on other carb-restricted diets like Atkins, Keto, and Paleo.

Contrary to popular opinion, carbohydrates are unnecessary, so humans can survive without them and still operate typically. But that doesn't necessarily mean we are made to survive without them.

In contrast to other well-liked weight loss programs, a carnivore diet focuses only on food choices and rarely makes advice regarding calorie or macronutrient targets or meal timing.

CARNIVORE DIET MEAL PLAN

Eating could get a little monotonous, given the simplicity of the diet and its list of permitted foods. But it doesn't have to be that way.

For you to better understand the diet, we've created a special 7-day Carnivore Diet meal.

THE FIRST DAY

Carnivore **Breakfast** Tacos with Machaca con Huevos
Patties made from ground beef for **Lunch**
Sardines as a **Snack**
The **Dinner** menu for the first night is NY strip steak

THE SECOND DAY

The **Breakfast** menu includes pork shoulder steaks
Tuna and hard-boiled eggs for **Lunch**
Beef jerky Old Fashioned Original by People's Choice as a **Snack**
The menu for **Dinner** included a rack of lamb and bone broth

THE THIRD DAY

The **Breakfast** menu consists of eggs and bacon
The **Lunch** menu consists of bone broth and roasted chicken
Hard-boiled eggs as a **Snack**
The **Dinner** of the day was pork shoulder confit

THE FOURTH DAY

Steak and eggs for **Breakfast**
Pork chops roasted for **Lunch**
The People's Choice Carne Seca Machaca Jerky Chew is the perfect **Snack**
Turkey burgers for **Dinner**

THE FIFTH DAY

Eggs and pork sausage for **Breakfast**
Bison burgers for **Lunch**
Pate and pork rinds as a **Snack**
Prime Rib for **Dinner**

SIXTH DAY

A lamb omelet for **Breakfast**
Bacon and chicken breast for **Lunch**
Tuna as a **Snack**
Steak ribeye for **Dinner**

SEVENTH DAY

A **Breakfast** of chicken livers and eggs
Patties made from ground beef for **Lunch**
The **Snack** of the day is grilled chicken tenders
Confit chicken legs and bacon for **Dinner**

CARNIVORE DIET BENEFITS

Although the carnivore diet's veracity is heavily contested, there is no denying that many give it credit for significant improvements.

Losing weight

A strict meat diet will help you lose weight more quickly because you're switching from using carbohydrates as your primary energy source to fats. This is like the ketogenic diet.

When you are fat-adapted, sometimes referred to as being in ketosis, your metabolism can use food and body fat stored as fuel. This implies that you can use your body fat as fuel to burn off.

Protein and fat are also incredibly satiating. Studies have also indicated that gaining weight enhances your hunger hormones, further managing your appetite. You may go for several hours without thinking about eating.

Heart Wellness

Vitamin K2 is abundant in meat and has been found to reduce artery calcification, significantly contributing to the onset of heart disease.

A high-protein diet may also help lower levels of LDL, also known as "bad cholesterol," according to a 2019 review.

Some people may increase their cholesterol levels when consuming large amounts of animal meat and fat. However, the overall effect will be good for heart health due to considerable reductions in inflammation and glucose/insulin surges.

Glucose sensitivity

A low-carbohydrate diet may also improve insulin sensitivity (Silva, 2014). Your body's ability to move glucose from your bloodstream into cells for energy is known as your insulin sensitivity. Thus, eating like a carnivore could help maintain stable blood sugar levels and lower your chance of acquiring diabetes.

Both autophagy and inflammation may be reduced with its help.

Limiting calories and carbohydrates can lower inflammatory levels and encourage autophagy (the natural process of cell repair and damage cleanup). If a person experiences chronic inflammation and weight loss, this may substantially affect their general well-being.

But remember that eating lots of protein daily will inhibit autophagy. You might not fully experience these effects from a carnivorous diet if intermittent fasting is not included.

Simple eating style

It is simple to incorporate a carnivore diet. The foods made from animal origins are well known. Eating a diet entirely composed of meat can be an excellent approach to start dieting if you have a hectic schedule and frequently get confused about macronutrients, calories, meal scheduling, and preparation. Even though it may be expensive, meat is known to be highly filling, so you will feel full for a very long time.

Boost in Testosterone

Diets rich in healthy fats have been demonstrated to raise testosterone levels since they are essential for hormone function, including testosterone.

Most people will consume more protein and good fats on the carnivore diet, which could increase energy, power, and muscle mass. Don't worry if you're a lady, either. Your hormones, including testosterone, will be regulated by the extra fat rather than raised.

Mindfulness

Numerous carnivores have reported feeling more energized, focused, and mentally clear. The lack of carbohydrates, developing a fat-adapted body, and reliance on ketones (fats) as an energy source are probably to blame for this.

According to studies, ketones have neuroprotective qualities, and the brain prefers fats to carbohydrates for energy.

It might lessen autoimmune disease-related symptoms.

Most food allergies and sensitivities are eliminated when one adopts a meat-only carnivore diet. This may aid the body in recovering from persistent immunological reactions brought on by plant-based diets.

Better Gut

Several plant foods cause gastrointestinal disruption. While generally good, fiber can also give you gas and bloating. Nightshades (potatoes, eggplants, peppers, and tomatoes) contain proteins called lectins that can irritate the stomach. Numerous fruits include phytochemicals like flavonoids and tannins that can irritate the stomach. You might have fewer digestive problems if you cut out plant-based foods. Remember that a significant diet change like this will likely result in initial digestive side effects (like any other change of this magnitude).

It might be beneficial for digestive problems brought on by specific plant diets.

The Carnivore diet consists of easily digested meals and leaves little waste behind. The symptoms of inflammatory bowel disease and irritable bowel syndrome brought on by plant fibers and other substances may benefit from this low-residue diet.

The main components of meat are protein and fat, which are absorbed in the small intestine and don't leave anything behind to aggravate or swell the gut. This may allow the gut to heal and regenerate.

However, it is unknown how an all-meat diet will affect the microbiome and gut health over the long run.

Usually, the carnivorous diet encourages ketosis.

For most people, the carnivorous diet is likely to cause nutritional ketosis. Nevertheless, consuming too much protein has been shown to inhibit the creation of high ketone levels.

We advise adopting a keto-friendly strategy if you want to try carnivorism because ketosis has several unique advantages beyond what a carnivore diet can offer.

IS EATING LIKE A CARNIVORE HEALTHY?

Over the past five years, social media has highlighted the carnivorous diet. Former orthopedic physician Dr. Shawn Baker and Dr. Paul Saladino, who have hundreds of thousands of internet followers and have participated on the Joe Rogan podcast, are our supporters.

Studies on carnivorous diets reveal improvements in markers of chronic diseases, psychological problems, autoimmune conditions, and weight loss, despite the lack of study in this area.

Self-reported data, like surveys, are a fragile type of evidence. Surveys can be used to develop hypotheses and guide future research, but they shouldn't be used to make decisions about your lifestyle.

There is little to no evidence of the long-term consequences of a diet that entirely excludes plant foods while having specific nutritional components and supporting weight loss, such as accessible elements from foods sourced from animals and high-quality protein.

Some of the beliefs held by the carnivore group have elements of truth, like the notion that vegetables carry anti-nutrients (such as phytates in lentils, which block the absorption of iron) and that humans evolved to consume meat.

The problem arises when these findings are stretched to support wildly improbable conceptions of reality.

Plants may have anti-nutrients, but it doesn't mean they don't also possess health-enhancing qualities that balance these impacts. Even though we may have evolved to eat meat, this does not imply that we only consumed meat throughout our evolution or that we followed a low-carb diet.

Many nutrients and minerals, like calcium and vitamin C, are under scrutiny for not being consumed enough. Our gut health, an organ that frequently depends on the by-products of carbohydrate and fiber digestion, may also be negatively affected.

Since many carnivores' diet followers report high cholesterol levels, heart disease is another worry. It is difficult to determine whether this poses a long-term health risk without additional factors, including high blood pressure, smoking, and type 2 diabetes.

While we can consult stories from Arctic communities like the Inuit, case studies, surveys, and anecdotal data, we're mostly left to make assumptions about physiological systems for how the body might handle the conditions brought on by a carnivore diet.

Although highly resilient and adaptable, human physiology is, nonetheless. Furthermore, some people who follow the carnivore diet may be healthy, provided it can give all the necessary nutrients. What is optimal vs. what is only possible, nevertheless, differs.

We don't rely on guesswork or ban entire food groups at Second Nature. With the aid of a qualified dietitian or nutritionist, we offer evidence-based advice to assist you in reaching your health goals.

Are people intended to live solely on meat?

There is ample proof that humans evolved to eat meat. Hominin (a prehistoric human progenitor) sites have been discovered that show butchery and tool use as far back as 1.5 million years ago. At the same time, further data points to a likely age of almost 3 million years ago.

Did this affect our evolution?

It has been hypothesized that more excellent meat, fat intake, and foraged plants allowed the human brain to expand and develop. The gut shrank as the brain grew more extensive because it was no longer required to process such enormous volumes of fibrous plant material.

According to research, mammals cannot have giant versions of the gut and the brain because they are both energy-intensive organs. For instance, compared to humans, monkeys typically have smaller brains.

Nevertheless, because their diet has remained predominantly plant-based, they have retained their more enormous gut, particularly the colon, which is roughly twice as big as ours.

It is evident that meat played a role in our evolutionary history, but does this indicate that humans have evolved to eat only meat?

Even though meat was a part of our diets, there isn't any proof that we had a strict meat-only diet.

According to research, the time of year and the place we eat greatly influence our diets.

We occasionally followed a low-carb, high-protein diet; other times, a high-carb or perhaps a diet high in fat to induce ketosis. As opportunistic omnivores, our predecessors consumed a variety of macronutrients and consumed what was available to us.

This notion is supported by research on contemporary hunter-gatherer societies. In Tanzania, East Africa, there is a hunter-gatherer tribe known as the Hadza.

According to studies, they eat many meat and plants, especially wild game, honey, berries, and tubers. Contrary to popular belief, the Hadza have low cardiovascular disease and body fat rates.

This does not imply that the Hadza diet is the best for humans to consume. Simply put, they consume what is available to them in their surroundings.

We have the luxury of having access to many meals in modern rich nations. Thus, we are no longer limited by seasonality and geography. As a result, there is more variety and a lesser chance of vitamin deficiencies.

It is assumed that our predecessors followed a particular diet when it is suggested that we follow their example because that is how we developed to eat when it was a necessity-based diet.

Do any plants have toxicity?

The idea that plants may contain toxins bad for humans is a central tenet of the carnivore movement. Plants have evolved compounds to protect themselves from being eaten because they lack the physical defenses that animals rely on, such as teeth and antlers.

This statement has some validity, just as there are too many nutritional ideas. Lentils, for instance, provide non-heme iron but also contain phytic acid (phytates) that prevents the mineral from being absorbed by the body.

However, over our species' existence, we've learned how to enhance the nutritional content of various foods and the bioavailability of critical nutrients.

It has been proven that anti-nutrient content can be reduced, and the bioavailability of minerals like iron and calcium can be increased using cooking, milling, soaking, and fermentation.

Phytic acid levels in lentils were found to drop dramatically during the boiling and soaking processes. A separate study found that soaking chickpeas for up to 12 hours can reduce their phytic acid concentration by up to 55%.

Some potentially toxic chemicals in plant meals have significantly been decreased or eliminated thanks to selective breeding and improved agricultural practices.

The claim that plants have anti-nutrients is valid, yet humans have discovered means to increase the nutritional content and digestibility of plant-based diets throughout history.

Plant-based diets have beneficial health effects.

Diets rich in plant foods like fruits, vegetables, nuts, seeds, and legumes have been shown to improve health, regardless of biochemical reactions. A lower incidence of obesity and other chronic diseases like type-2 diabetes has been linked to a diet higher in plant foods.

This will still be the case if nothing else in your diet changes. Two variations of the traditional American diet (usually heavy in ultra-processed and low in plant foods) were studied to determine their effects.

The first group was told to keep eating as they usually would, whereas the second was given the same advice but told to increase their fruit and vegetable intake by four servings per day.

Those who increased their intake of fruits and vegetables lowered their blood pressure, whereas those who did not experience any change.

This implies that even a slight increase in fruit and vegetables consumed can improve physical health indicators.

Potential deficiencies

It is possible that diets that restrict entire food groups, such as the vegan and carnivore diets, may raise the risk of micronutrient deficiencies and negatively influence our health over the long run.

This is not to indicate that you won't be able to get all the nutrients you need on these diets; instead, it just means that it will be more difficult for you to get all of the nutrients you need because the variety and choice of foods in your diet will be restricted.

Some people, for instance, limit their diet to just steak and eggs, which is one example of the variation that can be found in the carnivorous diets that people follow. Any additional restrictions on what may be considered an already limited diet will undoubtedly heighten the danger of nutritional deficiencies.

Vitamin C

Vitamin C is a crucial vitamin that the body needs to maintain a healthy immune system and facilitate the healing of wounds. The number of foods that contain vitamin C from animal sources is relatively low, whereas the number of foods that contain vitamin C from plant sources is high.

A study examining the availability of several nutrients in a carnivore diet found that beef tongue was the best source of vitamin C, with 1.3 milligrams per one hundred grams. In addition to being possible sources of vitamin C, fish roe and liver can also be consumed.

As a rule, a daily intake of at least 40 milligrams (mg) of vitamin C is recommended. Although the needs of each person are unique, if we were to assume that 40 mg was the optimal target, then you would need to ingest three kilograms of beef tongue daily.

Interestingly, case study reports of people who ate a carnivorous diet for an entire year did not exhibit any clinical indications of scurvy (vitamin C deficiency). Although it hasn't been scientifically confirmed, the carnivore diet is said to reduce the amount of vitamin C that a person must consume daily.

It is unknown whether this would lead to health problems as no studies have explored this over a long period. Vitamin C pills are something that people who follow a carnivorous diet should probably think about taking.

Fiber

Even though fiber is not a required food for human existence, it is commonly believed to be helpful for our health since it helps to promote the operation of our gastrointestinal (GI) tract and the diversity of the microbiota that live in our gut (bacteria).

What kind of effects will a diet devoid of fiber have on our digestive tract?

Studies have indicated that eliminating fiber from the diet in those who suffer from diseases such as irritable bowel syndrome (IBS), IBS-like symptoms, or small intestinal bacterial overgrowth

(SIBO) can provide symptomatic relief in the short term and lead to an improvement in bowel movements.

After following a carnivore diet for four weeks, five of the six individuals diagnosed with SIBO tested negative for the presence of the bacterium that causes SIBO. Research has also indicated that reducing the amount of fiber consumed can have a short-term beneficial effect on constipation, bloating, and flatulence symptoms.

In contrast, research indicated that persons treated with extra fiber reported experiencing improvement from these symptoms in 77 percent of cases. It has been hypothesized that although cutting back on fiber intake or eliminating it can alleviate symptoms in the short term, it might not necessarily treat the illnesses that are the root cause.

The digestive tract's health depends on various factors and is not solely determined by fiber consumption. There will be a part to play in the quality of our nutrition. Overall, the amount of sleep we get, the amount of activity we get, and our mental health.

Because there has only been a small amount of research done on the long-term effects of a diet lacking in fiber on our gut and overall health, it is currently unknown whether you would develop health difficulties in the long run if you followed such a diet.

TIPS THAT CAN SAVE YOU MONEY WHILE STAYING ON THE CARNIVORE DIET

It could appear challenging to follow the carnivore diet on a limited budget.

The cost of meat is high. There is no avoiding it at this point. However, following the Carnivore Diet does not require spending much money on food. The Carnivore Diet can be customized to match any financial plan if one is strategic in grocery shopping and uses their imagination.

These tips and tactics will assist you in saving money, regardless of whether you are just starting or are an experienced pro.

Beef jerky from the Carnivore Diet is an excellent method for cutting costs while satisfying a craving for meat.

Take less expensive cuts of meat.

If you choose the appropriate cuts of meat, you can make significant financial savings. There is a significant cost differential between the various portions of the meat.

Who among the carnivorous species doesn't enjoy a good ribeye steak? However, other solutions are less expensive.

The prices of some of the most common cuts of beef are detailed in the following list. Because demand, supply, and trends all impact pricing, you shouldn't be hesitant to try purchasing more expensive pieces of meat because prices might vary greatly depending on these factors.

Maintain a ready shopping list with the less expensive cuts of beef to capitalize on any deals at your neighborhood market.

Spend on beef of lower quality.

You can save even more cash by choosing beef of lower quality. There is no correlation between the grading of meat and food safety or even the quality of the meat.

The United States Department of Agriculture (USDA) assigns ratings to individual cuts of beef depending on the marbling or fat level. The presence of marbling in a steak helps to improve its flavor, softness, and juice content. Select, Choice, and Prime are the three different beef grades available. A portion of meat given the Prime classification has been deemed to have the highest amount of marbling.

It should not be inferred from this that lower-grade beef lacks quality or flavor. Knowing how to cook these more resilient cuts of meat properly is the key to success. A Select cut of beef can be transformed into Prime quality by braise cooking at a low and slow temperature.

If you're having trouble, turn to ground beef.

On the Carnivore Diet, consuming ground beef is the most cost-effective method to reap the advantages of beef without breaking the wallet.

Ground beef is a convenient and adaptable protein option. Please place it in a frying pan and cook it over high heat for a speedy dose of beef. You may also include it in eggs or create burgers and meatballs. On the Carnivore Diet, hundreds of different recipes call for ground beef.

Ground beef is the workhorse of the Carnivore Diet for those on a limited budget since it can be quickly frozen, defrosted, and cooked.

Choose animals that are given grain rather than grass.

The price of grass-fed beef is typically anywhere from 50 to 100 percent higher than grain-fed beef. When compared to other feeding methods, grain-fed animals offer significant cost savings.

Even though there are advantages to grass-fed beef, eating any beef is preferable to not eating any meat at all. If the choice is between grain-fed beef and no meat, grain-fed beef will invariably emerge victorious.

Combine more inexpensive ingredients in the dish, such as eggs, sardines, and cow organ meats like the beef liver.

Eggs that were produced on pasture in a basket.

The Carnivore Diet is not limited to the consumption of meat solely. There is a diverse selection of food products that are derived from animals that can also be incorporated into your everyday routine.

Eggs are the best choice available. They provide many elements lacking in beef muscle, such as choline, vitamin K2, vitamin E, and selenium, which are made up for by these foods. When you can, try to find eggs reared on pasture because they have a higher nutrient content.

Seafood that has been preserved in a can is another affordable alternative. The most widely consumed variety is tuna in a can; however, you can also choose from canned salmon, sardines, mackerel, herring, or anchovies. These are nutrient-dense powerhouses that offer an incredible amount of benefits. Omega-3 fatty acids, vitamin D, and iodine are all abundant in canned fish. Be cautious about purchasing choices that are packaged in water rather than oil.

Beef offal is another less conventional choice. The kidney, the liver, and several other organs have an extraordinarily high concentration of various nutrients, including protein, vitamins, and minerals. These more daring items could make some people queasy, but for those who aren't afraid to try new things, they offer a lot of bang for their buck.

Buy meat while it is on sale.

A meat counters stocked with several cuts of steak. Local food stores frequently run sales. Be sure to stock up on your go-to items as soon as they are made available.

Saving money on workhouse cuts like ground beef or chuck roll, for example, can be accomplished by this method quite easily. Additionally, it is a beautiful method to indulge in the more expensive cuts without completely emptying one's bank account.

Get to know the butcher at your neighborhood store. They can assist you in locating cuts that are not as widely used and hence cost less. They might also provide discounts on cuttings that they want to sell quickly. If you tell them that you follow the carnivore diet and lifestyle, they may be more willing to assist you.

Do not hesitate to take advantage of meat markdowns and offers about to expire. When you buy meat that has been marked down because there is a possibility that it could go bad soon, you can make significant financial savings. You should anticipate reductions ranging from 25 to 75% of the original price.

When in doubt, go straight to the source.

You can acquire beef by going straight to the farm or ranch where it was raised. You can find farmers and ranchers by searching the local area or going to a farmers' market.

Although ranchers need to place larger orders, the cost savings should make it worthwhile. Your leftover meat can permanently be frozen for later use.

You can also save money by using an online service that delivers meat. These subscription firms work with local ranchers to provide customers with various meat selections that may be purchased directly from the company. You will save money if you eliminate the need for a middleman in the transaction.

Shop at big box or warehouse stores to make bulk purchases.

Costco, Sam's Club, Walmart, Restaurant Depot. Proceed to any of your preferred neighborhood wholesale establishments.

Do you run your own company? Applying for a free membership is simple when shopping with wholesale restaurant shops like Restaurant Depot.

Do not be afraid of the refrigerator.

Frozen beef that has been wrapped. You can preserve your savings by putting them in the freezer when you buy in large quantities. Meat frozen correctly can remain edible for anywhere between six and twelve months.

When storing meat in the freezer for an extended period, vacuum-sealing it is the most effective method for maintaining its freshness.

Use a variety of different sources of protein in rotation.

Although beef has the most nutritional value for those following the Carnivore Diet, this does not preclude consuming alternative forms of protein.

On the Carnivore Diet, popular alternatives include chicken, hog, lamb, and deer; the diet also allows for the consumption of unusual meats such as elk and buffalo.

Prepare the dish using bone-in cuts.

In terms of cost per pound, bone-in cuts of meat are less expensive than boneless cuts. Even though they contribute some mass, the meat is far heavier than the bones. Because they need less work to process, steaks with the bone still in them are sold at a lower price point.

The connective tissue and fat surrounding bones significantly contribute to the dish's flavor and nutritional value. They also assist in ensuring that specific cuts of beef cook in an even manner.

Prepare a broth from the bones.

You may make homemade bone broth with the bones left over from cooking cuts that include the bone. To prepare a snack or supper high in various nutrients, boil the bones in water.

Bone broth is a simple meal that can be made on the Carnivore Diet that is versatile enough to be enjoyed throughout the year. You can enjoy the carnivore bone broth or include it in a braising dish.

Eat 1-2 substantial meals a day.

The Carnivore Diet encourages shorter fasting periods and minimizes binge eating frequency. On the Carnivore Diet, you will rapidly learn that you need to consume fewer meals per day and fewer meals overall.

A diet consisting solely of meat helps you feel fuller for longer. The high levels of fat and protein in the diet send the message to your body that it is satisfied with its current state of fullness. On the Carnivore Diet, many individuals claim that they do not require any snacks and do not feel the need to eat three meals per day. Instead, they consume one or two very huge meals per day.

This will ultimately consume fewer calories and save money in the long run.

CARNIVORE DIET COST

There is no requirement that the Carnivore Diet be pricey. The exclusionary character of the Carnivore Diet can save you money in the long run if you plan and do your shopping strategically. As an illustration, let's look at how much money you need to spend to follow the Carnivore Diet if you exclusively consume ground beef.

Let's say that the daily calorie requirement for the average person is about 2,500.

There are 240 calories, 21 grams of protein, 17 grams of fat, and 0 grams of carbohydrates in a serving size of four ounces of 80/20 ground beef. To meet your daily calorie requirement of 2,500, you must consume approximately 10.3 servings of ground beef.

This equates to almost 2.5 pounds of ground beef consumed every single day.

The price of retail ground beef across the country averages $4.33 a pound. On the Carnivore Diet, the recommended daily consumption of ground beef is 2.5 pounds, which results in a cost of $10.83 per day due to the price of beef, which is $4.33 per pound.

If one followed a conventional diet, that sum of money wouldn't even come close to covering lunch. You can save even more money by implementing some of the additional strategies for cutting costs that were suggested before.

THE TOP ADVICE FOR PEOPLE FOLLOWING A CARNIVORE DIET

If you are thinking about attempting the carnivore diet, there are a few things you need to know beforehand. The following advice, supported by scientific research, should be followed to ensure that the carnivore diet benefits your health.

About how much protein should one eat in a single day?

The recommended daily allowance (RDA) for protein consumption is 0.8 grams per kilogram of body weight. The National Institutes of Health established the RDA.

This is the bare minimum amount that must be consumed to fulfill your fundamental dietary needs. This indicates that you can consume more protein, but not less.

Proteins are essential for developing blood, connective tissues, antibodies, bones, enzymes, and many other bodily components, including those listed above.

You may need more protein if you compete in sports or grow muscle.

The carnivore diet is a high-protein diet, which means you will consume sufficient and even additional healthy protein to fulfill all your body's needs nutritionally. Compared to plant diets, animal products such as fish, poultry, and beef have higher protein content.

How to Get Enough Vitamin C in Your Carnivore Diet and What to Do About It

Vitamin C is a crucial nutrient for maintaining good health; its antioxidant activity prevents various health issues.

Meat, fish, poultry, and eggs, in addition to dairy products, all offer enough vitamin C, an essential nutrient for the body.

Although foods containing meat do have vitamin C in them, it is essential to take precautions when preparing them. Vitamin C can be destroyed through prolonged cooking in significant volumes of water or exposure to air for extended periods. Because hydroxyproline and hydroxylysine are utilized in the process of collagen formation in a carnivorous diet, these organisms have a reduced need for vitamin C.

You can increase the amount of vitamin C in chicken and fish by marinating them in lemon juice if you still feel like you need it. Taking vitamin C supplements is another option available to you.

How can one incorporate vegetables into their diet if one eats meat primarily?

A person who follows a strict carnivore diet does not include vegetables in their daily food intake.

If you follow a modified version of the carnivore diet, you'll be able to consume only small portions of various vegetables, like avocado, lettuce, mushrooms, and cucumbers.

Because it helps to lessen the acidic effects that eating meat can have on blood, nutritionists and other experts believe that including some fiber-rich vegetables in one's diet should always be considered beneficial and healthy. These vegetables may facilitate improved digestion of foods derived from animal sources. You can eat them in salads or meat and vegetable curries.

What should be done to obtain fiber and nutrients?

The carnivore diet provides all the necessary nutrients to maintain health. You may have constipation if you switch to a diet high in meat and other animal products. This is because your body requires time to adapt to the new eating pattern.

A carnivore's diet contains a more active form of nutrients that are also highly bioavailable and absorbable than the diet of a plant eater. Compared to foods made from plants, those made from meat have the lowest levels of inflammation.

Many experts believe fiber is necessary for improved digestion and more effective waste disposal. However, some reports lowering the amount of fiber consumed helped minimize the symptoms of bloating and gas. According to one piece of research, increasing dietary fiber consumption is linked to increased stomach pain and bloating levels. Constipation and stomach pain can be made significantly worse by insoluble fiber. According to the study's findings, cutting back on fiber consumption effectively alleviates the symptoms associated with constipation.

Physical activities to be participated in while following the carnivore diet

A healthy lifestyle includes regular physical activity, such as running, yoga, meditation, and cardio workouts. During the adaptation phase, you may experience fatigue because of the keto flu or a modification in the pattern of your food. After an initial period of adjustment, a carnivore diet can assist in the development of muscle and abdominal definition.

It could take up to a month for your body to adjust to the diet and lifestyle of a carnivore. After you sense that your body has adjusted, you can begin your regular physical activity regimen. Because exercise makes your body more insulin sensitive, it can be a very beneficial addition to the carnivorous diet. If you want to lose weight more quickly, combining the carnivore diet with exercise will help you accomplish this objective more effectively.

Who should avoid eating meat?

Even if the carnivore diet has all the necessary nutrients, it might not be the best choice for some subsets of the population.

Since persons with chronic kidney disease are required to restrict the amount of protein they consume, it is not recommended for these individuals.

Consuming foods high in cholesterol should be approached with caution if you are hypersensitive to the effects of cholesterol or if you are a cholesterol hyper responder. Therefore, it is in your best interest to steer clear of the carnivorous diet because of the increased fat you will take in.

Because children, women who are pregnant or nursing, and nursing mothers require more and a wider variety of nutrients, this product is not advised for them. Despite this, there are a lot of testimonies out there that claim the carnivorous diet is the greatest one for breastfeeding and pregnant women.

If you have health issues such as diabetes, high blood pressure, or obesity, you should probably talk to a medical practitioner before making significant alterations to how you eat. On the other hand, fish meat is abundant in the mineral magnesium and omega-3 fatty acids, which contribute to a reduction in blood pressure.

If you suffer from food phobia or have trouble controlling how much you eat, the carnivore diet is not the right choice for you to make. Before beginning this diet, you must discuss your health concerns with your primary care physician or another healthcare provider. To monitor your nutritional condition, your physician may suggest that you undergo specific tests.

The consumption of alcohol while on the carnivore diet

If you follow a strict carnivore diet, you won't be able to include any carbohydrates in your meals. Whiskey, gin, rum, wine, vodka, and tequila are some examples of pure types of alcohol that, when consumed in moderation, do not contain a significant amount of carbohydrates. These can be consumed on their own, mixed with water or other low-carb beverages such as lemon water or mint water for added flavor, or taken directly from the bottle.

Alcohol consumption slows down the development of ketosis and influences the outcomes of a carnivorous diet. On rare occasions, you are allowed to consume one portion of alcohol.

The various and preferred methods of ingesting meat

A carnivore's diet consists of meats such as cattle, lamb, organ meats, turkey, chicken, hog, and fish such as salmon, sardines, and whitefish.

You can season the dish with a bit of salt and pepper and add a small amount of cream and hard cheese. Your diet could also benefit from adding butter, lard, and bone marrow.

It is strongly suggested that you consume organic meat because it is very nutritious and tasty. It is crucial to ensure that your body receives all the necessary nutrients. If you are starting and find it challenging to consume organic meat, try mixing it with ground beef dishes like meatloaf or hamburgers. Explore the possibility of purchasing meat from organic animal farms; compared to conventional livestock; organic meat possesses a higher nutritional value.

You should avoid eating processed beef because it has a higher chemical content, which is terrible for your health. The carnivore diet encourages using simple cooking techniques to maintain good health. Consuming raw meat on a carnivore diet is not recommended because it destroys many of the nutrients that can be found in cooked meat.

The carnivore diet does not emphasize daily calorie consumption, the number of individual servings, the number of meals, or the number of snacks consumed. It advises avoiding beverages such as tea and coffee and recommends drinking more water or bone broth to keep yourself well-hydrated.

DO'S AND DON'TS ON A CARNIVORE DIET

DO'S IN CARNIVORE DIET

Maintain a healthy level of hydration: Increase the amount of water, bone broth, meat soup, and other refreshers that you drink to stay hydrated. It is essential to consume more electrolytes while on a diet.

Regular exercise and other forms of physical activity help you maintain your health and get better results. It is essential to make a habit of eating every part of the animal, from the head to the tail; you should also avoid skipping organ meat because it is as healthful and nutritious.

Consume between one and three meals daily, ensuring that the meat is well cooked and avoiding processed meat if possible.

Because organic cattle are better cared for, getting organic meat is better than getting meat from conventional livestock.

Engage in a test that lasts for thirty days: If you are thinking about switching to a carnivorous diet, you should participate in a 30-day challenge. Your body requires time to adjust to the zero-carb diet to realize results such as weight loss and general fitness level improvements.

Eat only the egg whites or reduce your egg consumption if you have a sedentary lifestyle.

DON'TS OF A CARNIVORE DIET

If you are on a carnivore diet, you should avoid drinking carbonated drinks because they include carbohydrates; otherwise, you could not obtain the results you seek from your diet.

Avoid drinking alcohol. On the other hand, you might want to think about mixing your strong liquor with water occasionally.

If you are pregnant, lactating, a diabetic patient, a cardiac patient, or you are suffering from kidney difficulties; then you should not put too much pressure on yourself to stick to the diet. You should seek the advice of your physician to determine whether your current state of health allows you to adhere to a carnivorous diet. Eat until you are completely satisfied, but don't worry about counting calories; the carnivorous diet gets its energy from fat.

It is recommended that you steer clear of eating any fruit alongside your meal if you want to avoid experiencing bloating.

GUIDELINES FOR EXERCISING WHILE FOLLOWING A CARNIVORE DIET

These suggestions are for anyone who aims to increase their lean muscle mass while reducing their overall body fat percentage. If that doesn't describe you, these rules don't apply to you! Whether your primary objective is to improve your athletic performance, become as strong as possible, or do something else, these aspects of your training should be adapted accordingly.

Do heavy compound lifts

The squat, the deadlift, the bench press, the overhead press, the barbell row, pullups, and bar dips are all compound movements. These lifts work multiple muscles simultaneously. These are not workouts you receive a pump from; you should put most of your attention into developing your strength with them. They lay the groundwork for your physique, which serves as a support system for the rest of your training.

They also have a significant effect on hormones! According to several studies, squats and deadlifts are two of the best exercises for releasing anabolic and growth hormones. This indicates a decrease in body fat and an increase in muscle! Study the form for them and work your way up gradually. Lifting heavy objects is an excellent way to preserve bone density, mobility, and overall muscle mass as you age.

Compared to performing separate isolation exercises for each muscle group, pulling pull-ups will work your shoulders, biceps, and forearms in addition to your lats. Better bang for your buck!

15-minute daily calisthenics

A full-body bodyweight workout that takes 15 minutes is an excellent option for people who are extremely busy or who detest going to the gym.

This will work your complete body, so be sure to include jump squats, pushups, pullups, bridges/superman, leg raises/flutter kicks, alternating jump lunges, and possibly handstand pushups or mummy walks in your routine. Doing one set to failure on each of these exercises is sufficient. In addition to that, I strongly suggest getting a pull-up bar and a jump rope.

Zone 2 cardio

When doing cardio in zone 2, you want to keep your heart rate at 180 minus your age, which is your target heart rate. When performing cardio in zone 2, I try to keep my heart rate in the 150s as much as possible. This guarantees that I will burn fat rather than sugar as my primary fuel source.

This looks like brisk walking, mild jogging, hiking, swimming (for certain people), cycling, Stairmaster, and elliptical machine workouts.

I prefer to exercise about thirty to forty-five minutes in zone 2 every day to help promote fat loss and enhance my aerobic fitness.

Keeping glycogen reserves low allows more to be used when lifting high weights. It is also much simpler to recover from and places significantly less stress on the body. In addition, HIIT will not stimulate your hunger in the way that Zone 2 cardio can.

Limit glycolytic exercise!

High-intensity interval training, Tabata, Crossfit, sprint intervals; your boxing cardio class; your spin cycle class. All of these are wonderful; however, they have an extremely high rate of glycogen (sugar) consumption in the muscle.

This can stimulate your appetite, deplete the central nervous system, cause you to feel sore, and wear you out! Keep your high-intensity cardiovascular training to once or twice per week. Or, if you want to be leaner, have more energy, and keep your appetite in check, you should limit the duration of your workout to less than 15 minutes.

Add more salt to it!

Electrolytes can be quickly lost with a larger workout volume, particularly if the individual is fasting and sweating. Make sure you get plenty of salt in your diet to prevent cramps and protect your thyroid at the same time.

When I want a good workout, I sometimes have a cup of black coffee with a teaspoon of salt.

Sleep!

It would help if you got enough to sleep to increase muscle mass, recuperate from workouts, and keep a fantastic hormonal profile. Weightlifting is a catabolic activity, which means that it breaks down your muscles. The anabolic effect of sleep is that it rebuilds them.

Because there are so many distinct factors involved, everyone behaves a little bit differently when it comes to sleep. For me, having a regular time to get out of bed each day is essential. I usually sleep between 6 and 7 hours on average.

Take in more protein!

When I do higher training volumes, I always find that increasing the amount of protein I consume is extremely useful. If you want to increase the size of your muscles, the anabolic response from eating more protein might be pretty helpful.

Chicken, beef, salmon, eggs, turkey, and bacon are all safe bets regarding food choices. Additionally, collagen protein is fantastic.

1.   RECIPES

1. BASICS

1.   CREAMY SHRIMP AND EGGS

INGREDIENTS

- Half a cup of unsalted butter
- One cup of chicken broth
- A pound of raw shrimp
- A quarter cup of grated parmesan cheese

INSTRUCTIONS

- The oven should be preheated to 350 degrees Fahrenheit. Butter and broth should be added to a saucepan and stirred well.
- Using a baking tray, place the shrimp on top of the butter mixture.
- Bake for 10 to 15 minutes at 350 degrees Fahrenheit, topped with parmesan cheese.
- Bake for 10 to 15 minutes at 350 degrees Fahrenheit, topped with parmesan cheese.

2. PIE WITH ORGANIC MEAT

INGREDIENTS

- Salt as needed
- Three eggs
- Tallow from beef
- There are half cups of ground beef tongue in this recipe
- Ground beef heart with quarter cups
- quarter cup ground chicken liver

INSTRUCTIONS

- This organ meat pie is a great place to start if you can't eat certain organ meats alone. This recipe combines ground muscular meat, heart, liver, and sometimes bone marrow to make a delicious 30-minute meal.
- Combine all the meat with some salt. In a skillet over medium heat, lightly brown the meat with fat.
- Place the meat mixture on a baking tray, add the eggs, and bake for 45 minutes.
- Prepare an oven to 350°F and bake the mixture for 15 minutes. Slice it after it has cooled.

3. AIR FRYER MEATBALLS

INGREDIENTS

- One and a half pounds of ground grass-fed beef
- Two eggs
- Snack bag of pork rinds, 1.5 ounces
- Three ounces of shredded cheese.
- a pinch of salt
- One tablespoon of lard

INSTRUCTIONS

- Make balls by rolling the combined ingredients into a big ball.
- Air-fry the meatballs for 8-12 minutes at 360°F.
- Turn them halfway through the cooking process to ensure the balls cook evenly.
- The meatballs are done when they reach an internal temperature of 165 degrees Fahrenheit.
- I enjoy how the meatballs in this meal are mixed with crushed pig rinds instead of regular breadcrumbs.

4. 10-MINUTE SKILLET SHRIMP

INGREDIENTS

- Peeled and deveined medium shrimp weighing one pound
- 1 Tablespoon Ghee or other fat for cooking
- 1 tsp. of salt
- 2 tbsp. of shredded Parmesan cheese (optional)

INSTRUCTIONS

- Wash and dry the shrimp.
- Melt cooking fat in a large skillet over medium heat.
- Put the shrimp in the pan. About seven minutes later, give the pan a good toss after the shrimp have turned pink and are cooked through.
- Sprinkle some cheese on top, then season with salt. Give everything a good stir. To be served hot.

5. CARNIVORE PIZZA

INGREDIENTS

- A teaspoon of salt
- Approximately 400 grams of pork ground
- There should be 200 grams of beef liver
- Three large eggs
- Bacon 50 grams
- Mozzarella 50 grams

INSTRUCTIONS

- Set your oven's temperature to 175 degrees Fahrenheit.
- To make a smooth consistency, mix the beef liver in a blender. Mix the ground pork with the liver, eggs, and seasonings in a bowl, then spread it evenly on the pizza pan's bottom.
- Please put it in the oven for 15 minutes or until the bacon is crisp. Take the casserole out of the oven and sprinkle the chorizo, mozzarella, and bacon over the top.
- Cook for another 5-10 minutes.

6. CHICKEN NUGGETS

INGREDIENTS

- A chicken thigh weighing 14 ounces
- The quantity of scratching and crackling pork is 5 ounces
- Two medium eggs
- One teaspoon of black pepper

INSTRUCTIONS

- Cubed chicken can be added to beaten eggs with freshly cracked black pepper. Coat the nuggets with egg, then roll them in the ground pork-cracking mixture.
- The nuggets need to be baked for 15–20 minutes in an oven to 400 degrees Fahrenheit.
- When I make them at home, I like to accompany them with sour cream or barbecue sauce.

7. CARNIVORE CASSEROLE

INGREDIENTS

- Ground beef, one-half cup
- Two eggs, a quarter cup of full-fat cream
- 1/4-pound cream cheese
- One pinch of salt

INSTRUCTIONS

- Combine the ground beef with the eggs, cream, and cream cheese. Add some salt to taste, then throw it in a 350°F oven.
- Slice it after baking for 25-30 minutes.

8. HERBY BONE BROTH

INGREDIENTS

- A couple of pounds of meaty bones
- 8 cups of water
- Two tablespoons of apple cider vinegar
- One tablespoon of sea salt

INSTRUCTIONS

- Put everything in an instant pot and cook on high pressure for 2 hours. Once the broth has cooled, drain it using a sieve.
- Extra broth can be stored in the refrigerator or frozen in an airtight container.

2. BREAKFAST

9. CARNIVORE WAFFLES

INGREDIENTS

- Two eggs
- Quarter cups of uncooked breakfast sausage
- Oil extracted from coconuts

INSTRUCTIONS

- Crack the two eggs into a bowl and mix them into the sausage. The sausage can be broken into smaller pieces for equal cooking in the waffle maker.
- Spray some Coconut Oil Spray onto the waffle maker.
- The waffle iron should be preheated before you add the mixture. Keep in the oven for 3 to 4 minutes.
- Warm in a 200°F oven on a baking sheet lined with paper towels.

10. CARNIVORE BREAKFAST SANDWICH

INGREDIENTS

- The sausages should be two patties
- One egg
- Grease from bacon
- The American cheese

INSTRUCTIONS

- The butter should be melted in a large skillet over medium heat. Make sausage patties approximately the size of your palm but no more than half an inch thick. Brown patties on one side, flip, and continue cooking for another 2–3 minutes.
- If you don't mind the flavors blending, you can fry an egg and some bacon in the same skillet. If you don't have enough butter, always use a second skillet (medium heat, and wait until the pan is hot to prevent sticking) and cook the meat separately before assembling your meat eater's breakfast sandwich. Use the liquid yolk as a sauce.
- Assemble the dish by placing one sausage patty on a platter and topping it with a fried egg, cheese, and a second sausage patty.
- Enjoy! You can also add sliced avocado, tomato, or cooked spinach.

11. BUTTER BAKED COD

INGREDIENTS

- Salt 4 fillets of cod (about 6 ounces each)
- grass-fed butter or ghee, ¼ cup

INSTRUCTIONS

- The oven is recommended to be preheated at 400 degrees Fahrenheit (204 degrees Celsius).
- Sprinkle salt on the fish on both sides.
- Put into a baking dish (like a glass pyrex). On top of each fillet, smear one tablespoon of butter or ghee.
- Fish should be flaky when poked with a fork after 20 minutes in the oven.
- After plating the fillets, use a spoon to drizzle the pan sauce over the top. Quickly and hotly serve.

12. BROILED SALMON FILLETS

INGREDIENTS

- Four salmon fillets, wild-caught
- melted 1/4 cup ghee
- salt

INSTRUCTIONS

- Make a flat glass or enamel plate a catchall for your fillets. Coat each piece with cooking butter and brush to distribute evenly.
- To prepare a broiler, heat the oven.
- Arrange fillets so that they are three inches below the heat source. Submit to the broiler for around 6 minutes. Gently turn over, and if necessary, add more butter and a brush. Increase the broiling time by 4 minutes. Sprinkle some salt on it, and serve it hot.

13. SHRIMP TACOS

INGREDIENTS

- The Monterey Jack cheese should be shredded into 1 cup
- Colby cheese, shredded, ½ cups
  For the Shrimp
- ½ tablespoons of butter or ghee made from grass-fed animals
- Peeled and deveined ten medium shrimp

INSTRUCTIONS

How to Assemble Taco Shells

- First, have a 350F (175C) oven ready.
- Prepare a baking sheet with parchment paper and a rim.
- Third, in a separate bowl, mix the various kinds of cheese. Make six cheese circles on the tray, each measuring 4 inches in diameter. Please put it in the oven and brown it for about 5 minutes.
- Taco "shells" should be formed using a spatula when the cheese has nearly cooled. Turn the circles so that the sides that were previously facing down are now facing up. Make sure you round them up while they're sitting and cooling off.
- Shrimp tacos in a warm, crunchy shell topped with gooey melted cheese are perfect for brunch, lunch, or dinner. They look great on the table for a pre-dinner snack and are fun to eat while standing around the kitchen island.

Prepare the shrimp in one of two ways.

- Cook the shrimp over medium heat in half a tablespoon of butter or ghee. It should take around 7 minutes or until the meat turns pink.
- Once they're cool, cut them up into smaller pieces.

The Purpose of This Gathering Is To Serve

- Split the shrimp between the taco shells relatively in a hot dish.

14. CHEESE-STUFFED SALMON SANDWICHES

INGREDIENTS

- Half a cup of room-temperature Country Home Cream Cheese
- 1/4 cup Organic ricotta cheese,
- Four salmon fillets, skinless and boneless
- Salt

INSTRUCTIONS

- First, have a 350F (175C) oven ready.
- Prepare a baking sheet with parchment paper and a rim.
- Next, combine the cream cheese and ricotta in a separate basin.
- Four, with the skin side down, place two salmon fillets on the baking sheet.
- 5-Spread the cheese mixture on both fillets in an even layer.
- Add the remaining fillets, skin-side up, to the dish in step 6. Douse with salt.
- Please put it in the oven for 20 minutes or until the salmon is fully cooked. In a hot dish.

15. CARNIVORE QUICHE BREAKFAST MUFFINS

INGREDIENTS

- 8 ounces of Grounded beef
- The rinds of pork
- Nine large Eggs
- Raw cheese
- One teaspoon of Sea salt
- Sage is optional
- Nutmeg is optional.
- Rosemary is optional
- Thyme is optional
- Chives is optional

INSTRUCTIONS

- To bake successfully, preheating the oven to 375 degrees is required.
- Prepare the dough for the beef-and-pig-rind pie crust.
- The pork rinds should be ground into a powder in a blender. Make room in your mixing basin for the powdered pig rinds.
- The pig rind powder must be seasoned with sage, thyme, nutmeg, rosemary (if used), and salt. Combined, they make a great mix.
- Puree the raw ground beef and eggs in a blender until you have a homogeneous mixture.
- Put the beef-egg paste in a bowl and knead it into a dough.
- Use a muffin tin to shape the crusts.
- Prepare crusts from the dough and press them into the bottom of the cupcake slots in the baking pan. For an illustration of this, please refer to the "Tips to make the best..." section.
- Prepare the crusts in the oven.
- To make the crust, put it in the oven for 20 minutes at 375 degrees.
- Prepare the egg-cheese filling as the crusts bake.
- Whisk together the six eggs in a large mixing basin. Using a hand mixer is acceptable, but it's not required.
- Get a mixing bowl and a cheese grater, then shred the raw cheese right into it. Combine the cheese with the eggs by folding it in and seasoning with a pinch of salt.
- You should complete it.
- Take the crusts out of the oven when they're done baking. Put some of the egg and cheese mixtures in each pie crust.
- Be aware that it is common for some of the fillings to spill out of the slot's center and into its sides. A single muffin is the result of the combined ingredients.
- Bake at 375 degrees for 15 to 20 minutes to get a golden brown top.
- If using, sprinkle some chopped chives over the top before baking.
- As soon as the muffins are done baking, take them out of the oven and let them cool for about 10 minutes.

- Refrigerating leftovers in an airtight container extend their shelf life to four to five days.

16. PROTEIN PANCAKES

INGREDIENTS

- Protein powder containing 50 grams of whey
- Cottage cheese 100 g
- Three large eggs
- A teaspoon of baking powder
- One tablespoon of butter

INSTRUCTIONS

- While I could happily maintain a carnivore diet on a steady diet of beef alone, I find that sprinkling in the occasional indulgence helps keep things interesting.
- My pre-workout breakfast for the past few months has been these pancakes.
- Combine all the ingredients in a blender and blend until thick paste forms.
- Then, brush the pan with oil and heat it over medium before adding the batter in increments. Flip the pancake and cook for another 40-45 seconds.
- These delicious carnivore pancakes are a great way to start the day because they are keto-friendly and made with cottage cheese, two ingredients known for their high nutrient density.
- It's also highly flexible, so play with different flavors by adding or subtracting components.

3. RED MEAT, PORK AND POULTRY

17. CARNIVORE BRAISED SHORT RIBS

INGREDIENTS

- A total of four pounds (about eight ribs) of short ribs
- For seasoning, use a generous amount of salt
- Alternatively, one tablespoon of garlic sauce could be used
- Chicken broth in the amount of two cups

INSTRUCTIONS

- Ensure that the short ribs are heavily salted on all sides. If the short ribs rest for at least 30 minutes, the salt can penetrate the meat more effectively. Bake the chicken at 325° for about 25 minutes.
- Cook with fat in a large Dutch oven over medium heat (lard, tallow, duck fat, or whatever you choose) until it's warm and hot. 3–4 short ribs should be added, and the crust should be golden brown for 1–2 minutes on each side. When containers are too close together, steam can form. Work in batches to avoid this. Short ribs' natural juices and flavors will be preserved by steaming.
- If desired, add garlic sauce to the Dutch oven with the short ribs. After pouring in the chicken bone broth, bring it to a boil. You should remove the rib meat from the fire and bake it at 325 degrees for 1.5 to 2 hours after it has peeled away from the bone.

18. GARLIC-BUTTER STEAK

INGREDIENTS

- 3-4 pound one beef flat iron steak
- 1/8 teaspoon salt
- 1/8 teaspoon pepper
- Two tablespoons butter, softened, divided
- One teaspoon minced fresh parsley
- 1/2 teaspoon minced garlic
- 1/4 teaspoon reduced-sodium soy sauce

INSTRUCTIONS

- Combine one tablespoon each of butter, parsley, garlic, and soy sauce.
- Sprinkle salt and pepper on the steak. Cook the remaining butter in a large skillet over medium heat. Cook the steak for 4-7 minutes per side or until it reaches your preferred doneness (medium-rare should register 135 degrees Fahrenheit on a thermometer; medium-well should read 145 degrees). Serve with garlic butter.

19. CARNIVORE FRIED CHICKEN STRIPS

INGREDIENTS

- Thighs of chicken
- Pork cracklings, pork rinds, or pork rinds are also good options.
- The egg
- Salt of the sea

INSTRUCTIONS

- Create the breading first.
- Put the pork cracklings in a blender and whirl them around until they resemble an oily powder.
- In the interest of full disclosure, pig rinds will also work, although I could not get a thick breading coating.
- Put the powder for the pork cracklings in a large basin.
- Next, get the chicken strips ready.
- Slice the chicken thighs lengthwise. I sliced mine into 4-inch-long by 1/2- to 1-inch-wide strips, but you can make them as big as you like.
- Prepare the chicken strips for frying.
- In a little bowl, whisk together two eggs.
- To prepare chicken strips, dip them in an egg wash. Dip it into the crackling pork powder and roll it around until it is completely covered. The oiliness of the powder will help it to clump. Take care to bread the item thoroughly.
- Prepare a baking sheet with parchment paper and add the coated chicken strips. Douse them in salt.
- After 20 minutes in the oven at 400 degrees, turn the food over and bake for another 20 to 25 minutes. The completed chicken strips will have a firm and crunchy coating to the touch. These turned out great, thanks to 20 minutes in the air fryer at 400 degrees.
- Dish it up, then dig in! Get creative with your dipping sauces and whip up some Onion-Free Guacamole, Honey Mustard, or Duck Fat Ranch Dressing.
- To save them for later, place them in an airtight container and keep them in the fridge for no more than two days.

20. OVEN-ROASTED WHOLE CHICKEN

INGREDIENTS

- An organic whole chicken weighing five pounds
- ¼ cups softened butter or duck fat
- A tablespoon of salt

INSTRUCTIONS

- Bring the temperature of your oven up to 425 degrees Fahrenheit (218 degrees Celsius).
- Use frying fat to coat the chicken. Season generously with salt.
- Spread in a baking dish and bake for 1 hour or until the internal temperature reaches 165F (74C). When done, the exterior will be golden and crispy.
- Take the dish away from the heat and let it sit for ten minutes before serving.

21. SALTED DRUMSTICKS

INGREDIENTS

- There are 12 organic chicken drumsticks.
- 1/4 cup fat, melted (butter, ghee, tallow or lard)
- Granulated ocean salt

INSTRUCTIONS

- The oven needs to be heated to 450 degrees Fahrenheit (230 degrees Celsius).
- To prepare, place parchment paper on a baking sheet with a rim.
- In a bowl, mix the drumsticks with the two tablespoons of oil.
- The drumsticks need to be baked for about 30 minutes or until they are completely done. Baste with the remaining two tablespoons of cooking fat halfway through the cooking time.
- Add salt to taste. Put it under the broiler for five minutes to warm the skin in a hot dish.

22. PULLED PORK

INGREDIENTS

One cup of broth, either bone or chicken

A pork butt weighing three pounds

One tablespoon salt

INSTRUCTIONS

The slow cooker should be set at its lowest setting. Mix in some pork butt and broth. Douse with salt.

Cover and cook on low for 8-12 hours or until pork is tender enough to shred with a fork.

Put the pork on a serving platter and shred it using two forks.

Incorporate additional fat (butter, olive oil, etc.) and serve hot—place leftovers in the refrigerator.

23. CRISPY PORK BELLY

INGREDIENTS

- Approximately 12 pork belly slices (12 inches thick, every 4 ounces raw)
- A teaspoon of salt

INSTRUCTIONS

- The oven is recommended to be preheated at 400 degrees Fahrenheit (204 degrees Celsius).
- Set out a large piece of parchment paper on a baking sheet with a rim. Spread the strips out and season them with salt.
- Start by roasting for 30 minutes, flip each piece and roast for another 30 minutes or until brown and crispy.
- Take it off the stove, and set it aside to cool. Remove the fat and store it in a jar for later use.
- Prepare either hot or cold.

24. CARNIVORE STROGANOFF

INGREDIENTS

- Approximately 300 g of lean ground beef
- One-fourth cup of full-fat cream
- salt

INSTRUCTIONS

- Prepare the oil by heating it in a pan or skillet over medium heat.
- Slowly add the ground meat and heat until it browns.
- Then, add the heavy cream and a pinch of salt.
- The liquid should be reduced by half while simmering.
- Please put it in the fridge to cool down and serve.

25. BEEF PATTIES WITH ONION GRAVY

INGREDIENTS

- 500 g of beef is a pound
- One stick of butter
- Exactly 4 tbsp flour 1 tsp salt 1 tbsp chopped onion
- 1-cup chicken stock
- Chemical compounds used as seasonings

INSTRUCTIONS

- Put some salt and other seasonings on the steak in the pot. Blend the flour in carefully. Go away for a couple of hours.
- Form the meat mixture into patties and set them aside.
- The butter needs to be melted and the pan heated.
- Put in all the patties and fry them up.
- The food should be moved to a serving plate.
- Put some onion slices in the pan and some broth.
- Repeat this process until the gravy thickens.
- When ready to serve, pour the sauce over the burgers.

26. CHICKEN LIVER PATE

INGREDIENTS

- One tablespoon parsley
- ½ teaspoon salt
- One shallot
- ¼ teaspoon black pepper
- 500g chicken liver
- ½ cup butter
- Two cloves of garlic

INSTRUCTIONS

- In a skillet, melt the butter. Roast the garlic and sweat the shallot.
- Brown the chicken liver on both sides in a pan until it is soft. Toss in some parsley.
- Season with salt and pepper, then stir in the remaining butter.
- To crush the components, stir slowly. The meal should be poured into a container and cooled for some time.
- Accompany with bread.

4. FISH AND SEAFOOD

27. CARNIVORE CRAB DIP

INGREDIENTS

- One lb. of crab meat, lump
- 1 cup softened Country Home Cream Cheese
- Half a teaspoon of salt

INSTRUCTIONS

- The oven needs to be heated to 450 degrees Fahrenheit (230 degrees Celsius).
- Prepare a mini baking dish by coating it with butter.
- Mix the crab meat, cream cheese, and salt in a bowl.
- Put in a baking dish and bake. Put in the oven and set a timer for 30 minutes. Incorporate heat when serving.

28. EASY SEARED SALMON

INGREDIENTS

- 1/4 cup ghee, divided
- 6-ounce fillets of wild-caught salmon
- 1/2 teaspoon salt

INSTRUCTIONS

- The oven needs to be heated to 450 degrees Fahrenheit (230 degrees Celsius).
- Set a cast-iron or oven-safe pan over medium heat and add the butter. Just a pinch of salt, please, and mix it in.
- When the oil is hot, put the salmon fillets' skin-side down. Turn after one minute of searing and continue cooking for an additional minute.
- Then, put the skillet in the oven and add two teaspoons. Set the oven timer for 8 minutes in a hot dish.

29. STEAMED CARP

INGREDIENTS

- 1 (4- to 5-pound) whole carp
- Hot water

INSTRUCTIONS

- Fish must be cleaned and scaled before cooking.
- To prepare, place the rack over boiling water (use a DIY setup or a turkey roaster).
- The water must be brought to a boil and then covered securely. Fish is done when it flakes readily when tested with a fork, usually after about 25 minutes at a low simmer.
- Offer at a comfortable serving temperature.

30. SAUTEED ABALONE STEAKS

INGREDIENTS

- 3/8-inch thick abalone steaks
- ¼ cup Ghee
- Salt

INSTRUCTIONS

- Use a wooden mallet to pound the steaks to a thickness of about a quarter of an inch.
- Prepare a skillet with melted butter or ghee over medium heat.
- Add abalone steaks to the butter for 30 seconds on each side and cook.

Put some salt on it. Make sure to serve right away.

31. BOILED SNOW CRAB LEGS

INGREDIENTS

- 2 pounds frozen snow crab legs
- Hot water
- One teaspoon salt
- Ghee

INSTRUCTIONS

- Add enough water to a saucepan, so the crab legs are entirely submerged. Put a teaspoon of salt into a pot of water and bring it to a boil.
- The cooking temperature should be decreased to a simmer before adding the clusters of crab legs. There should be roughly 8 minutes of cooking time left.
- Drain the water off the legs. Water can be removed by giving the container a light shake.
- Serve immediately while still hot with your choice of butter or ghee. You can add salt to the meat if it tastes bland.

32. BACON-WRAPPED SEA BASS

INGREDIENTS

- 12 uncured bacon strips
- Two tablespoons grass-fed butter or Heritage Pork Lard
- 4 (6-ounce) sea bass fillets

INSTRUCTIONS

- Turn the oven temperature to 375 degrees Fahrenheit (190 degrees Celsius).
- To prepare, place parchment paper on a baking sheet with a rim.
- Sea bass fillets should be brushed with cooking grease before cooking. You should use three pieces of bacon for each fillet and lay them on the sheet with the seam side down.
- The fillets must be baked for about 25 minutes or until they are flaky and cooked in a hot dish.

33. OVEN-ROASTED SWORDFISH WITH SMOKED SALT

INGREDIENTS

- Two tablespoons Ghee or cooking fat
- One teaspoon of smoked sea salt
- 2 pounds of swordfish steaks

INSTRUCTIONS

- Has an oven preheated at 350 degrees Fahrenheit (175 degrees Celsius)?
- Steaks of fish should be baked in an oven-safe dish. Cover the fish in frying grease and sprinkle it generously with salt.
- Fish of varying thicknesses should bake for about 20 minutes. When cooking fish, thinner fillets will finish faster than broader ones. After cooking, the fish is flaky and readily separated with a fork.
- Construct a heated plate and serve.

34. SURF 'N' TURF

INGREDIENTS

- 4 (6-ounce) haddock fillets
- 1 pound ground pork
- Ghee or Heritage Pork Lard

INSTRUCTIONS

- The oven is recommended to be preheated at 400 degrees Fahrenheit (204 degrees Celsius).
- Pork should be cooked in a cast-iron or ovenproof skillet over medium heat; the meat should be stirred often to prevent sticking. Keep going for another 5 minutes or until browned and fully cooked.
- Disperse the meat around the pan. Haddock fillets should be placed on the mixture, separated from one another. Brush the tops with frying grease.
- Put in the oven. In a preheated oven, cook fish for 12-15 minutes or until it flakes easily when tested with a fork. Incorporate heat when serving.

5. SAUCES AND SIDES

35. CARNIVORE-FRIENDLY WHIPPED CREAM

INGREDIENTS

- ½ teaspoon stevia tincture
- One teaspoon of vanilla extract
- 1 cup heavy whipping cream

INSTRUCTIONS

- Throw everything in a food processor with an "S" blade, as shown.
- To make gentle peaks in the cream, whip it in a mixer until the components thicken. You should set aside 2 minutes for this.
- Serve warm or refrigerate as a garnish for other Carnivore Diet sweets.

36. CARNIVORE-FRIENDLY NEW YORK CHEESECAKE

INGREDIENTS

- 8oz full-fat cream cheese
- 1.5 cups full-fat creme fraiche
- Four large eggs

INSTRUCTIONS

- Bake at 325 degrees Fahrenheit, the temperature at which you should prepare the oven. Set aside a buttered round cake pan. Prepare ahead of time by filling a big oven-safe container with water.
- Mix all of the above ingredients on medium-low speed in the bowl of a stand mixer outfitted with the paddle attachment.
- Put the ingredients in a greased cake pan, and bake for about an hour at 350 degrees Fahrenheit with a pan of water in the oven. This will keep the cheesecake moist and prevent it from cracking.
- You can spice up your cheesecake with some extracts or different sweeteners if you're not too picky. Enjoy!

37. CARNIVORE DIET BONE BROTH RECIPE

INGREDIENTS

- ¼ cup raw apple cider vinegar optional
- 6 pounds of beef bones

INSTRUCTIONS

- For 20 minutes, or until they reach a golden brown color, roast the bones in a single layer in a large roasting tray at 450 degrees Fahrenheit (232 degrees Celsius).
- A large stockpot is where the bones should be dumped. Fill the container with enough water to submerge the contents entirely.
- Put in some vinegar if you like.
- First, bring to a full boil, then reduce heat to a simmer. Cover the pot and bring the contents to a low simmer.
- Please don't take it out of the oven for at least 18 hours, preferably 72. I usually end the fermentation process after 24 hours. Maintain a constant water level above the skeleton. You can always add extra water if you need to.
- Make sure the broth is at a comfortable room temperature. A slotted spoon can easily remove the film or scum that forms on the surface. Strain the broth using cheesecloth or a fine-mesh strainer. Use glass jars to store your food for up to 5 days in the fridge and even longer in the freezer.

38. ANCESTRAL CARNIVORE VERSION

INGREDIENTS

- Two tbs of animal fat or butter
- One medium brown onion, thinly sliced
- salt to taste
- 400 grams of beef liver, diced
- Four strips of bacon, chopped into small bits

INSTRUCTIONS

- Until the bacon is crispy, cook it in a frying pan.
- To make caramelized onions, heat butter or fat until it foams, then add the onions and cook them until they are golden brown.
- Cook the liver for 2 minutes, stirring frequently.
- Prepare a dish, adding the fried bacon at the end.

39. SALMON WITH CREAM CHEESE SAUCE

INGREDIENTS

- 1/2 cup chicken stock
- salt
- 4 ounces of cream cheese
- pepper (optional)

INSTRUCTIONS

- Add all ingredients to a small spot and whisk at medium heat until combined and creamy.

40. GORGONZOLA CREAM SAUCE

INGREDIENTS

- One tablespoon of shredded Parmesan cheese
- Salt
- 1 cup heavy whipping cream
- 1 ounce of crumbled Gorgonzola cheese

INSTRUCTIONS

- Cook the cream until it just begins to boil.
- Allow the cream to boil, uncovered, for another 10 minutes or until it thickens. Time needs to be factored in if a recipe is increased in scale. The volume loss is expected to be roughly 1.5 times the starting point. Maintain constant stirring to prevent sticking to the pan and skin formation.
- Take it off the fire and mix in some Gorgonzola, Parmesan, and salt to taste. Add the cheese and stir it into the sauce until it melts.

41. GRILLED LOBSTER TAIL WITH TARRAGON BUTTER

INGREDIENTS

- 1 cup heavy whipping cream
- Salt
- 1 ounce of crumbled Gorgonzola cheese
- Shredded Parmesan cheese equaling one tablespoon

INSTRUCTIONS

- Bring the cream up to the point where it barely starts to boil.
- Cover and continue boiling the cream for 10 minutes or until it reaches the desired thickness. When scaling up a recipe, it's essential to account for the additional time needed. The predicted volume reduction is around 1.5 times the initial value. Keep stirring all the time to avoid burning and skin forming.
- Toss in some Gorgonzola, Parmesan, and salt to taste, then remove from heat. Toss the cheese into the sauce and mix it around until it melts.

42. CARNIVORE EGG PUDDING

INGREDIENTS

- 2½ tablespoons sweetener see note
- One teaspoon of vanilla extract
- One pinch salt
- Five soft-boiled eggs peeled
- 4 ounces half and half
- 1 tbsp softened butter

INSTRUCTIONS

- Put everything in a blender and whir it up until it's completely smooth. Try it out, and if it needs more sugar, add it.
- Chilling it in the fridge for at least two hours before serving is best.

6. NOSE TO TAIL

Recipes for Carnivore Diet Beef Brisket are shown here.

In this image, you can find the brisket part.

43. CARNIVORE DIET OVEN-BAKED BEEF BRISKET

INGREDIENTS

- Salt to taste
- 3-4 lb Beef Brisket
- Water

INSTRUCTIONS

- Bring oven temperature up to 275 degrees.
- Coat a large pan with cooking spray and add the beef.
- Fresh or frozen, liberally salt the brisket before placing it in the oven.
- Set a glass dish 8 inches by 8 inches full of water on the rack underneath the brisket to cook. This is a must if you want your brisket to stay juicy and flavorful!
- Cook your brisket in the oven until it is nice and tender (typically between 5-8 hours). A brisket cooked from frozen will take longer to prepare than one purchased at the store. Once the internal temperature hits 165 degrees, tent it with aluminum foil to hasten the cooking process (but this is optional). The brisket should be cooked to an internal temperature of about 205 degrees Fahrenheit, which is my preference (it starts to become very tender around 195-205). A meat thermometer will let you know if your brisket is cooked to the right degree. Depending on its size and thickness, brisket requires vastly different cooking times.
- Remove from the oven, cover, and rest for at least 20 minutes and up to 2 hours. Our briskets frequently spend time chilling in a portable cooler.
- Cut it up and eat it!

44. CARNIVORE BRISKET AIR FRYER RECIPE

INGREDIENTS

- 1 Tbsp Goat Butter
- 300 g Brisket
- Four large Egg Yolks
- 1 tsp Redmond Real Salt
- 1 Tbsp Beef Dripping, Also known as beef tallow

INSTRUCTIONS

- Slice the brisket thinly with a sharp knife and cut each slice into small cubes.
- Arrange the brisket in a single layer on the air fryer's base, and turn the temperature to 200 degrees Celsius. A large amount of salt should be applied to the meat. Start your clock in 10 minutes.
- Crack it open and rub the yolks and whites with your open palm over a dish to separate them. A lot of white people are going to miss out. In a separate bowl, add the egg yolks.
- Fry the yolks in the beef fat for a few minutes on each side over medium heat.
- Lay the meat and yolks out on a platter, sprinkle with more salt, and enjoy with cold butter. It's sure to be a delicious way to begin the day.

45. CORNED BEEF WITH CABBAGE

INGREDIENTS

- Three teaspoons of minced garlic
- One onion, sliced
- Salt
- 1 cup beef broth
- 1/2 head of cabbage, cut into 2" wedges
- 3-4 pound brisket
- One tablespoon peppercorns

INSTRUCTIONS

- **Slow Cooker Instructions:**
- It's best to use a lot of salt when seasoning brisket. Put the fatty side up in the slow cooker. Peppercorns, garlic, and onion pieces are poured over the meat. Cover the beef with liquid and sprinkle with salt again. Slowly simmer for 6 hours, add the cabbage wedges and continue cooking for another 2 to 3 until the cabbage and beef are fork-tender.
- **Instant Pot Instructions:**
- It's best to use a lot of salt when seasoning brisket. Put the fatty side up in the Instant Pot. Peppercorns, garlic, and onion pieces are poured over the meat. Add extra salt to taste, then pour liquid around the brisket. The Instant Pot must be covered, and the vent must be set to the "Sealing" position. Cook for 45 minutes on "Manual," or until the float valve has wholly fallen, letting Instant Pot finish the cooking cycle. Taking the brisket out of the pot requires lifting the cover. Put the cabbage in the pot, salt it, and cover it while ensuring the vent is sealed. For best results, while using the Instant Pot, it is best to select "Manual" and set the timer for 5 minutes. Reduce the thickness of the brisket slices. Turn the vent to the venting position and wait for the float valve to fall entirely before closing the vent. Take the lid off the Instant Pot and replace it with the brisket slices, covering them with the juices. Incorporate additional salt into the beef and cabbage before serving.

46. INSTANT POT BRISKET

INGREDIENTS

- Six cloves garlic smashed
- One tablespoon of tomato paste
- 1 (3 pounds) beef brisket, cut in half crosswise
- One teaspoon of ground pepper
- One teaspoon paprika
- Two teaspoons of extra-virgin olive oil
- One teaspoon salt
- 1 cup beef broth
- ¼ cup ketchup
- Two medium red onions, each cut into eight wedges

INSTRUCTIONS

- Salt, pepper, and paprika brisket. Multicooker Sauté setting (such as Instant Pot; times, instructions and settings may vary according to cooker brand or model). High-temperature setting; warm oil for 2 to 3 minutes. Add one brisket; cook for 7 minutes per side. Repeat with the remaining brisket. Stirring occasionally, sauté onions and garlic for 4 minutes to brown. Add broth, ketchup, and tomato paste to release browned chunks. Reheat the brisket. Stop.
- Lock the stove's lid. Seal the steam release handle. Press/Manual Preparation. Sixty minutes at high pressure. Before cooking, the pressure cooker needs 10 to 12 minutes to build. Let the pressure release naturally for 10 minutes. Turn the steam release handle to Venting before removing the lid (the float valve will drop; this will take 2 to 3 minutes).
- Rest the brisket for 10 minutes. Meanwhile, combine the onion mixture in the crockpot for 30 seconds.
- Discard the brisket's fat cap. Slice brisket against the grain and return to the sauce. Lock the stove's lid. Seal the steam release handle. Manual/Pressure Cook. 3 minutes high pressure. Before cooking, the pressure cooker needs 10 to 12 minutes to build. Let the pressure release naturally for 10 minutes. Turn the steam release handle to Venting before removing the lid (the float valve will drop; this will take 2 to 3 minutes). Serve brisket pieces with onion sauce.

47. PRESSURE COOKER "CORNED" BEEF & CABBAGE

INGREDIENTS

- 2 ½ pounds flat-cut beef brisket, trimmed
- Two tablespoons of ground pickling spice
- One small head of green cabbage (2 pounds), cut into eight wedges
- 2 cups low-sodium beef broth
- One medium onion, chopped
- One teaspoon of kosher salt divided
- Two tablespoons extra-virgin olive oil
- 2 pounds carrots, halved crosswise

INSTRUCTIONS

- Pickle meat with 1/2 teaspoon salt. Sauté oil in a pressure cooker—Cook the meat, rotating once, for 6 minutes total.
- Add onion and broth. Lock the cover. 40 minutes high pressure. Relax naturally.
- Stop. Leave the onion and liquid in the pot; remove the beef. On Sauté, add carrots, cabbage, and 1/2 teaspoon salt. Cook vegetables until soft and liquid are reduced by half, about 20 minutes.
- Served with veggies and drink, if desired.
- Combine butter and spicy sauce in a microwave-safe bowl. Melt sauce in the microwave for 20-30 seconds. Before serving, stir the fried chicken with sauce.

48. BRAISED BRISKET WITH CARROTS & PRUNES

INGREDIENTS

- 2 pounds beef brisket, preferably center cut, trimmed
- One teaspoon of ground coriander
- ¼ cup raisins
- One teaspoon salt divided
- ½ teaspoon ground pepper, divided
- Two medium carrots, chopped
- One teaspoon of ground cumin
- 1 cup low-sodium beef broth
- ½ cup chopped pitted prunes
- Two teaspoons of grated fresh ginger
- One tablespoon of grapeseed or canola oil
- One large, sweet onion, chopped
- Two cloves garlic, chopped
- One tablespoon of tomato paste

INSTRUCTIONS

- Dry the brisket and season it with a half teaspoon of salt and a quarter teaspoon of pepper. Turn on the Sauté setting on your electric pressure cooker and heat the oil. When the brisket has browned on all sides, about 8 to 10 minutes, flip it over. Move to a fresh plate.
- Put the onion, carrots, garlic, ginger, coriander, and cumin in the pressure cooker and cook for about 4 minutes, turning occasionally and scraping away any browned parts. Blend in the tomato paste, prunes, and raisins to the broth. Tuck the beef pieces into the gravy.
- Don't forget to secure the cover! Get an hour of high-pressure cooking done. Allow 15 minutes for the pressure to drop on its own. Manually releasing the residual pressure. Take off cover.
- Move the brisket to a cutting board that has been cleaned. The sauce needs the remaining 1/2 teaspoon of salt and 1/4 teaspoon of pepper stirred in. Serve the brisket with the sauce on thin slices cut against the grain.

49. STEAKY BEEF BRISKET NUGGETS

INGREDIENTS

- ½ cup cheese
- One big beef brisket steak
- One egg
- Three teaspoons oil
- One teaspoon of lime juice
- ¼ cup mayonnaise
- One teaspoon salt

INSTRUCTIONS

- Beef brisket steak, cheese, and salt should all be mixed. Combine harmoniously.
- To coat the steak mixture, beat an egg and place it in a container.
- Coat the steak pieces with the egg mixture by dipping them in it.
- Brown steak nuggets in a pan over medium heat.
- Sprinkle some salt and mayonnaise on the nuggets, then place them on paper rolls.

50. GRILLED BRISKET

INGREDIENTS

- Seasoning ingredients
- 3-pound beef brisket
- Two tablespoons smoked salt
- Four tablespoons butter

INSTRUCTIONS

- Thoroughly clean and dry the beef.
- Get the oven ready by preheating it.
- Be sure to liberally butter and season all sides of the chicken.
- Cook for around 40 minutes.
- Butter can be added if the beef has to be flipped. Put the dish back in the oven for another 40 minutes.
- Take it off the barbecue and rest for ten minutes before slicing.
- When ready to serve, arrange the grilled beef slices in a serving dish.

CONCLUSION

People looking for an alternative to the conventional ketogenic diet to reduce inflammation produced by meals, avoid food groups that cause digestion difficulties, or search for a more satisfying approach to lose weight are increasingly turning to the carnivore diet. Although the term "Carnivore Diet" makes it abundantly clear that the diet is predicated mainly on meat, there are a few nuances that you need to be aware of before commencing the diet. We will delve into detail and investigate the various possibilities available to prepare tasty meals while adhering to a carnivorous diet.

We do not know whether there are any distinct health benefits to following a carnivorous diet or whether the potential drawbacks have been exaggerated. We know that the carnivore diet encourages people to avoid foods scientifically proven beneficial to their health actively. Several studies have found that consuming a well-balanced, natural, and organic diet has many positive health effects.

Suppose you want to make significant changes to your diet to enhance your health. In that case, you should seek out and follow the recommendations of people you know and trust before embarking on a regimen as extreme as the carnivore diet. For instance, if you suspect that inflammation may be a problem, you should try an elimination diet that is more typical and still allows for the consumption of many regular foods rather than eliminating all items from your diet.

Made in United States
Troutdale, OR
09/16/2023